Ni~~ta Mehta's~~
P A
ALL THE WAY

Nita Mehta's

PANEER
ALL THE WAY

Serve a **new paneer dish** every time you call
your **old friends** over!

Nita Mehta

B.Sc. (Home Science), M.Sc. (Food and Nutrition), Gold Medalist

SNAB
Excellence in Books

Nita Mehta's PANEER All the Way

© Copyright 1994-2010 **SNAB** *Excellence in Books* Publishers Pvt Ltd

19th Print 2010

ISBN 978-81-86004-01-2

Food Styling and Photography: **SNAB** *Excellence in Books*

Layout and Laser Typesetting :

National Information Technology Academy
3A/3, Asaf Ali Road
New Delhi-110002
☎ 23252948

Published by :

SNAB Excellence in Books

Publishers Pvt. Ltd.
3A/3 Asaf Ali Road,
New Delhi - 110002
Tel: 23252948, 23250091

Distributed by :

NITA MEHTA BOOKS Distributors & Publishers

NITA MEHTA BOOKS
3A/3, Asaf Ali Road, New Delhi - 02

Distribution Centre:
D16/1, Okhla Industrial Area, Phase-I,
New Delhi-110020
　　　　Tel.: 26813199, 26813200
Bhogal: Tel.: 24372279

Printed by :
AEGEAN OFFSET PRINTERS

Editorial and Marketing office:
E-159, Greater Kailash-II, N.Delhi-48
Fax: 91-11-29225218, 29229558
Tel: 91-11-29214011, 29218574
E-Mail: nitamehta@email.com
 nitamehta@nitamehta.com
Website: http://www.nitamehta.com
Website: http://www.snabindia.com

Contributing Writers :
Anurag Mehta
Tanya Mehta
Subhash Mehta

Editors :
Sangeeta
Sunita

Recipe Development & Testing:

Nita Mehta Foods - R & D Centre
3A/3, Asaf Ali Road, New Delhi-110002
E-143, Amar Colony, Lajpat Nagar-IV
New Delhi-110024

Rs. 89/-

Introduction

■

P ANEER is the queen of dishes in every vegetarian home. The non-vegetarians too, shall be pleased with these recipes because they are in no way less in taste than their meat preparations.

When you call your friends over, you do want to prepare a paneer dish, but then you do not want to repeat the same paneer dish over and over again. The friends are the same but the paneer dish has to be different. So, here is a book which gives you a variety of new paneer dishes for your parties.

The Indian names of various ingredients have been used for convenience. However, their English equivalents are also given in brackets along with the Indian names.

I am grateful to my dear sister-in-law, Ravi Mehta, for always being helpful whenever I needed her during my book writing days.

Last, but not the least, I am thankful to my dear husband, Subhash, who is a constant source of inspiration to me.

Nita Mehta

With love to my dear son,

Anurag

whose great liking for paneer

inspired me to create these recipes

CONTENTS

■

ABOUT THE RECIPES

WHAT'S IN A CUP?

INDIAN CUP
1 teacup = 200 ml liquid
AMERICAN CUP
1 cup = 240 ml liquid (8 oz.)
The recipes in this book were tested with the Indian teacup which holds 200 ml liquid.

Snacks   **79**

NAMES OF INGREDIENTS

INDIAN NAME	ENGLISH NAME
Ajwain	Carom seeds
Amchoor	Dried mango powder
Anaardana	Pomegranate s
Atta	Whole wheat flour
Badaam	Almonds
Besan	Gram flour
Chillah	Pancake
Dalchini	Cinnamon
Dhania	Coriander
Dhania saboot	Coriander seeds
Garam masala	Mixed spices
Haldi	Turmeric
Hing	Asafoetida
Chhoti illaichi	Green cardamom
Imli	Tamarind
Kaju	Cashew nut
Kala-namak	Rock salt
Kali mirch	Black pepper
Kali mirch saboot	Peppercorns

Kalonji	Nigella seeds, Onion seeds
Kasoori methi	Dry fenugreek leaves
Kesar	Saffron
Khoya	Dried whole milk
Khus-khus	Poppy seeds
Kishmish	Raisins
Laung	Cloves
Magaz	Kernels of seeds of cucumber, melon, water melon and pumpkin mixed together
Methi dana	Fenugreek seeds
Moti illaichi	Brown cardamom
Nariyal	Coconut
Paneer	Cottage cheese
Pista	Pistachio
Poodina	Mint leaves
Saunf	Fennel seeds
Sirka	Vinegar
Suji	Semolina
Tej patta	Bay leaf
Til	Sesame seeds
Jeera	Cumin seeds

How to Prepare Paneer

Paneer is readily available in the market, but due to shortage of milk in summers, paneer becomes scarce in certain parts of our country.

To make home made paneer, it is important to use good quality milk. Paneer prepared from full cream milk is certainly softer and tastier than that made from skimmed milk available at MOTHER dairy booths.

To make paneer at home, take out juice of one lemon in a small bowl, carefully removing the seeds. The seeds taste bitter if they come in the paneer by mistake. If there is no lemon, keep one cup of curd ready.

Boil one kilo of full cream milk, stirring continuously to prevent skin forming at the top. When it comes to a boil, put off the fire. Add lemon juice or curd. Return to low heat, stir gently, till all the milk curdles and the greenish water called whey separates. Remove from fire. Leave it covered for 15 minutes. Strain through a muslin cloth and squeeze out the whey.

If cubes of paneer are required, keep the paneer which is wrapped in the muslin cloth in a rectangular ice cream box or an aluminium ice tray. The paneer takes its shape. To get a compact brick of paneer, place a heavy weight on the paneer for an hour or so. Remove the cloth and use the perfect home made paneer even when it is not available in the market.

Paneer as a Garnish

Last, but not the least, a dash of paneer here and there, enhances the taste and appearance of food. Paneer garnishes the food appetizingly.

Grated or diced (tiny cubes) paneer, when added to soups like tomato, vegetable or even hot n' sour, changes it for the better.

A simple mixed vegetable preparation can look exotic with a sprinkling of finely grated paneer. The white paneer enhances the colourful looks of the vegetables.

A simple bhatura, when filled with a spicy paneer filling, just a tablespoon - turns it into a special one.

The rest, I leave to your imagination.

Main Dishes

Paneer Tikka

Serves 4   *Picture on page 2*

1 capsicum - cut into fine rings
1 tomato - cut into long strips
2 onions - cut into fine rings
250 gms paneer - cut into big cubes
1 tbsp curd
1½" ginger piece, 3-4 flakes garlic
2-3 dried whole red chillies
½ tsp kala namak (rock salt)
½ tsp jeera powder (cumin seeds)
yellow colour - few drops
juice of ½ lemon
4 tbsp oil
1 tsp salt, or to taste

1. Cut paneer into 1½" cubes.
2. Grind ginger, garlic and chillies to a paste.
3. Mix curd, jeera powder, lemon juice, 2 tbsp oil, yellow colour, salt and kala namak to the paste.
4. Apply half of the paste on the paneer. Marinate for at least 1 hour, preferably longer.
5. Keep paneer pieces in a greased tray in a hot oven till the paneer gets well heated (15 minutes).
6. In a clean karahi put 2 tbsp oil. Add capsicum and onion rings. Cook till onions turn pink.
7. Add tomato strips, without pulp.
8. Add the left over ginger paste. Mix well for ½ minute.
9. Add a few drops of lemon juice.
10. Serve paneer surrounded by onions, capsicums and tomato strips.

■

Chilli Paneer

Serves 4   Picture on facing page

1½ tbsp cornflour
1½ tbsp maida (plain flour)
½ tsp salt
125 gms paneer
1½ tsp soya sauce
1 tbsp chilli sauce
2 tbsp tomato sauce
4-5 slit green chillies
4-5 flakes crushed garlic - optional
1 tbsp chopped coriander
¼ tsp each of ajinomoto and sugar
¼ tsp each of salt and pepper

Chilli Paneer ➤

1. Cut paneer into ½" cubes.
2. Mix cornflour, maida and salt in a bowl. Add enough water to make a batter of a thick pouring consistency such that it coats the paneer.
3. Dip each piece of paneer in batter and deep fry to a golden brown colour.
4. Heat 2 tbsp oil. Fry the green chillies and garlic. Reduce heat. Add salt, pepper, sugar and ajinomoto.
5. Add soya sauce, tomato sauce and chilli sauce.
6. Add the fried paneer and coriander. Mix well.
7. Cook for a few seconds till the sauces coat the paneer.
8. Serve hot.

■

Paneer Butter Masala

Serves 4-5

250 gms paneer (cottage cheese) - cut into big cubes
2 onions - chopped
1" piece ginger - chopped
6-7 flakes garlic
½ cup (100 ml) milk
4 big (250 gms) tomatoes
5 tbsp oil
1 tbsp kaju (cashewnuts) - broken into bits
2 tsp kasoori methi (dry fenugreek leaves)
3/4 tsp bhuna jeera (roasted cumin seeds) powder
1 tsp red chilli powder
1½ tsp salt, or to taste
½ tsp garam masala

¼ - ½ tsp sugar
1 green chilli - slit lengthwise
1 big capsicum - cut into thin shreds
2 onions - cut into thin rings
2 tbsp butter
few drops orange colour

1. Grind onions, ginger and garlic together to a paste.
2. Grind tomatoes to a puree.
3. Cook onion paste in oil, till golden (on the lighter side). Do not make it brown. Add red chilli powder. Cook for ½ minute.
4. Add milk gradually. Cook for 2-3 minutes.
5. Add kaju crushed on a chakla or powdered in a small grinder. Cook for 2-3 minutes.
6. Add tomatoes. Cook for 10-15 minutes on low flame till oil separates. Add jeera, garam masala, salt and sugar.

7. Add enough water, about 1½ cups. Cook for another 10-12 minutes till the oil separates and the gravy dries up to a thick masala gravy.
8. Add kasoori methi. Keep aside.
9. Heat butter in a clean karhai, add green chillies, capsicum and onions.
10. Saute for 2-3 minutes.
11. Add these vegetables to the prepared gravy.
12. Add paneer also.
13. Add colour. Keep on fire for 2-3 minutes.
14. Serve hot with nans or tandoori paranthas.

■

Shahi Paneer

Serves 4-5

250 gms paneer (cottage cheese) - cut into fingers
3 tbsp ghee
1 onion - chopped
½" piece of ginger - chopped
1 green chilli - chopped
4 big tomatoes - chopped
2 moti illaichi (brown cardamoms) - crushed
¼ cup beaten curd
1 tsp salt
¼ tsp red chilli powder
½ tsp garam masala
1 tbsp tomato sauce
1/3 cup milk or thin cream

1. Heat 2 tbsp of ghee. Add onion, ginger, green chilli and moti illaichi.
2. Cook until onion turns light brown.
3. Add tomatoes. Cook, covered, on low flame for 7-8 minutes.
4. Add curd. Cook for 3-4 minutes. Remove from fire.
5. Grind to a puree with ½ cup water in a liquidizer.
6. Strain the puree. Cook the tomato puree in 1 tbsp ghee for 5-7 minutes on low flame.
7. Add salt, chilli powder, pepper, garam masala and tomato sauce. Add enough water to get a thick gravy.
8. Boil. Keep on low flame for 5-7 minutes. Remove from fire.
9. At the time of serving, heat gravy and add paneer pieces.
10. Add cream or milk.
11. Serve garnished with a bunch of uncut coriander leaves surrounded by finely grated paneer.

■

Paneer Masala

Serves 4

250 gms paneer - cut into cubes
3 tbsp ghee
1 tsp ajwain (carom seeds) - crushed
2 big onions - chopped finely
1" piece ginger - chopped finely
2 green chillies - chopped finely
1 tsp garam masala
1 tsp red chilli powder
1 tsp dhania (coriander powder)
3/4 cup beaten curd
salt to taste

1. Cut paneer into 1½" x 1" rectangular pieces.
2. Heat 3 tbsp ghee, add 1 tsp ajwain crushed on a chakla-belan.
3. Add onions, green chillies and ginger. Cook till onions turn brown.
4. Add 1 tsp chilli powder and 1 tsp dhania powder. Mix well. Add paneer.
5. Blend in 3/4 cup beaten curd, salt and 1 tsp garam masala. Cook till curd dries up and ghee separates.

■

Good

made with no
bell pepper
Added
1 poblano
1 onion
used 1 can
Chopped tomatoes
no cilantro at end
used 1 t red pepper
flakes

Kadhai Paneer

Serves 6   Picture on facing page

250 gms paneer (cottage cheese) - cut into long fingers
2 capsicums - cut into long fingers
2 dry red chillies
1½ tsp saboot dhania (coriander seeds)
1½" piece ginger - chopped finely
1" piece ginger - finely shredded
10-12 flakes garlic - crushed
1 green chilli - chopped
2 tomatoes - chopped
a pinch of methi dana (fenugreek seeds)
1 tbsp chopped coriander
½ tsp salt, or to taste
4 tbsp oil

Kadhai Paneer ➤

1. Heat red chillies on a tawa, till slightly crisp and dry.
2. Pound (crush roughly) red chillies and saboot dhania on a chakla-belan.
3. Heat 1 tbsp oil in non-stick pan. Saute capsicums till done. Keep aside.
4. Heat 2 tbsp oil. Add methi dana and crushed garlic. Fry till garlic turns light brown. Add pounded dhania & red chillies. Cook for ½ minute.
5. Add chopped ginger and green chilli.
6. Add tomatoes, stir fry for about 5-7 minutes, on low heat till oil separates.
7. Add salt and capsicum. Stir to mix well.
8. Add paneer. Cook for 2-3 minutes.
9. Add shredded ginger and coriander. Mix well. Serve hot.

■

Mughlai Paneer

Serves 6

400 gms paneer (cottage cheese)
½ kg (6 big) onions - sliced finely
10-12 kaju (cashewnuts)
1 tbsp khus-khus (poppy seeds)
¼ cup fresh curd
2 tomatoes - blanched
½ cup milk
½ cup water (approx)
4 tbsp, 2 tbsp oil (6 tbsp)
1 tsp salt, or to taste
3/4 tsp red chilli powder
¼ tsp garam masala
oil for deep frying

1. Cut paneer into rectangular pieces of about ½" thickness.
2. Heat oil and deep fry the paneer to a light colour. Keep aside.
3. Soak khus-khus in 2-3 tbsp water for 15 minutes.
4. Heat 4 tbsp oil and fry onions till they turn golden brown.
5. Remove from fire. Grind to a wet brown paste with ¼ cup water.
6. Grind kaju and the soaked khus-khus to a wet white paste.
7. Heat 2 tbsp oil. Add the brownish paste and cook on low heat till golden brown in colour.
8. Add beaten curd and cook till the paste turns brown again. (3-4 minutes).
9. Put the tomatoes in boiling water for 2 minutes. Remove from water and peel the skin to blanch them.
10. Add the blanched, chopped tomatoes. Cook till oil separates. Keep mashing while cooking.
11. Add kaju paste and cook on low heat for 3-4 minutes.

12. Add milk and enough water to get a thick gravy.
13. Add salt, pepper red chilli powder and garam masala. Boil the gravy and simmer for 3-4 minutes.
14. Add the fried paneer. Serve hot.

■

Paneer Makhani

Serves 4   *Picture on page 1*

250 gms paneer (cottage cheese) - ½" thick, triangular pieces
3 tbsp ghee or 4½ tbsp oil
400 gms (7-8 medium) tomatoes - chopped
½" piece ginger - chopped
1 tej patta (bay leaf)
seeds of 2 moti illaichi (brown cardamoms) - crushed
1 tsp kasoori methi (dry fenugreek leaves)
½ tsp red chilli powder
1 tsp salt, or to taste
1 tsp or slightly more sugar
¼ tsp garam masala
5 tbsp (75 gms) cream or well beaten malai

1. Heat ghee in a karahi. Add tomatoes, ginger, tej patta, moti illaichi, kasoori methi and chilli powder.
2. Cook covered for about 10 minutes, till the tomatoes are pulpy.
3. Cool. Grind the tomatoes to a puree in the mixi.
4. Pass the puree through a fine sieve.
5. Keep the strained puree on fire. Add salt, garam masala and sugar to reduce the sour flavour.
6. Add 4 tbsp of cream. Remove from fire.
7. Add paneer pieces, about 1 hour before serving.
8. Garnish with swirls of beaten cream (1 tbsp), melon seeds, and coriander leaves.

■

Paneer Magaz

Serves 4-5

250 gms paneer (cottage cheese)
4 big (250 gms) tomatoes
1½ tbsp magaz
1 tbsp kaju (cashewnuts) - broken into bits
4 tbsp oil
2 tsp dhania (coriander) powder
salt to taste
¼ tsp garam masala
¼ tsp red chilli powder

1. Powder magaz and kaju by grinding them together.
2. Cut paneer into ½" cubes. Chop tomatoes.
3. Heat oil. Add tomatoes. Cook until oil separates.
4. Add the powdered kaju & magaz. Cook for 1-2 minutes.
5. Add enough water to make a gravy. Add salt to taste. Boil, simmer on low heat for 5-7 minutes.
6. Add paneer pieces. Remove from fire. Serve hot.

■

Saucy Paneer

Serves 4   Picture on facing page

250 gms paneer - cut into 1" cubes
1 large capsicum - cut into 1" pieces
1 large onion - cut into 1" pieces
1 large tomato - cut into 1" pieces
6-7 flakes garlic - crushed and chopped
2 green chillies - chopped finely
3 tbsp oil
1 tbsp soya sauce
1 tsp 8 to 8 sauce
a dash of tobasco or capsico sauce
1 tbsp chilli garlic sauce
1 tbsp tomato ketchup
½ tsp salt, or to taste

Saucy Paneer ➢

1. Heat 1½ tbsp oil in a non-stick pan or karahi.
2. Add capsicum and onion. Saute for 2-3 minutes.
3. Add paneer. Cook for 1 minute.
4. Remove pulp of tomato pieces and add to the paneer. Saute for a few seconds.
5. Remove all vegetables and paneer from the karahi and keep aside.
6. Heat 1½ tbsp oil in a clean karahi. Add crushed garlic and green chillies.
7. Add all sauces. Cook on slow fire for a few seconds.
8. Add the cooked vegetables and paneer.
9. Add salt and pepper to taste.
10. Cook for 2-3 minutes on low heat, sprinkling water occasionally, if required, till the sauces coat the paneer and vegetables.

■

Malaidar Paneer Kofta

Serves 4

250 gms paneer - grated
2 small boiled potatoes - grated
2 tbsp maida (plain flour)
2 green chillies - finely chopped
1 tbsp chopped coriander
salt to taste
½ tsp garam masala
1 tbsp malai
15-20 pieces of kishmish (raisins)
2-3 tbsp cornflour

CURRY
2 tbsp freshly grated or desiccated coconut
2 big onions - chopped

1 green chilli - chopped
1 dry red chilli - broken into pieces
½ tsp jeera (cumin seeds)
½" piece ginger - chopped
1 tbsp khus-khus (poppy seeds)
1 tbsp kaju - broken into bits
1 tsp dhania powder
2 tbsp ghee
2 small tomatoes - pureed
3-4 tbsp cream
¼ tsp garam masala
½ tsp salt, or to taste

1. Grate boiled potatoes. Add paneer, maida, green chillies, coriander, salt and garam masala.
2. Make 15-20 balls of potato - paneer mixture.
3. Flatten each ball, put a drop of malai and one kishmish in each ball.

4. Cover the malai with the potato mixture to from a ball again.
5. Roll each ball in dry cornflour or maida.
6. Deep fry 2-3 koftas at a time. Keep aside.
7. Heat ghee. Reduce heat. Add coconut, onions, green and red chilli, jeera, ginger, poppy seeds, kaju and dhania powder together. Cook till onions turn light brown. Grind all together in a mixer.
8. Heat 2 tbsp of ghee. Add onion paste and fry on low heat till paste is golden brown and ghee separates.
9. Add tomatoes pureed in a liquidizer. Cook for some time until ghee separates.
10. Add 1 cup water. Give 3-4 boils. Add salt & garam masala.
11. Keep on low heat for a few minutes.
12. Add cream. Mix. Add koftas. Remove from fire after ½ a minute till the koftas are heated through. Serve immediately.

■

Paneer Korma with Pineapple

Serves 4

250 gm paneer - cut into 1" rectangular pieces & fried till golden
½ cup shelled peas
2 slices of tinned pineapple - cut into 1" pieces
2 small carrots - cut into round slices
4-5 french beans - cut into ½" diagonal pieces
2 onions - chopped finely, 4 tbsp oil
¼ tsp haldi (turmeric) powder, ½ tsp garam masala, 2 tsp salt

GRIND TOGETHER (CASHEW-CURD PASTE)
4 tsp khus-khus (poppy seeds) - soaked in warm water for 30 minutes and drained
¾ cup curd, 2 tbsp cashews (kaju)
2 tbsp grated coconut (fresh or desiccated)
2 whole dry red chillies, ½" piece ginger, 3-4 flakes garlic
2 tsp saboot dhania saboot
seeds of 2-3 chhoti illaichi (green cardamom)

1. Soak khus-khus and drain. Grind it along with kaju, coconut, red chillies, ginger, garlic, saboot dhania and chhoti illaichi together to a paste along with curd.
2. Cut paneer into 1" cubes and deep fry till golden.
3. Heat 4 tbsp oil. Add chopped onions. Cook till onions turn golden. Add haldi. Stir to mix well.
4. Add kaju paste. Cook on low heat for 3-4 minutes.
5. Add beans, peas and carrots. Stir for 2 minutes.
6. Add 1 cup water or enough to get a thick gravy. Boil.
7. Add garam masala and salt. Simmer for 5 minutes.
8. Add paneer and pineapple. Boil for 1 minute. Serve.

■

Paneer Pasanda

Serves 4

200 gms paneer - cut into fingers
3 tbsp desi ghee
1 onion - chopped
1" piece ginger - chopped
1 green chilli - chopped
5-6 flakes garlic - crushed
3-4 laung (cloves)
3 chhoti illaichi (green cardamoms) - roughly crushed
1 small carrot - chopped
2 tsp kasoori methi
2 tsp maida dissolved in ½ cup water
3/4 tsp each of salt red chilli powder
¼ tsp sugar
½ tsp garam masala

½ tsp roasted jeera (cumin seeds) powder
1 cup water
4 tomatoes - chopped

1. Heat 2 tbsp ghee. Add onions, ginger, garlic, green chillies & laung. Cook till onions turn transparent.
2. Add carrots and crushed green cardamoms. Cook for 1 minute.
3. Add tomatoes & cook covered on low heat for 5-7 minutes.
4. Add 1 cup water. Boil. Keep on low flame for 2-3 minutes. Remove from fire and cool.
5. Blend in a liquidizer and strain the tomato gravy.
6. Heat 1 tbsp ghee. Add kasoori methi. Cook for ½ minute.
7. Add the strained tomato gravy. Cook for 5-7 minutes on low flame. Add maida paste, salt, sugar, red chilli powder, garam masala and jeera powder. Cook for a few minutes.
8. Add paneer pieces and serve hot.

■

Vegetable Paneer Kofta

Serves 8   Picture on facing page

1 carrot - shredded on the grater
1 capsicum - shredded
3-4 tbsp shredded cabbage
1½ tbsp oil
salt and pepper to taste

COVERING
250 gms paneer (cottage cheese)
1 bread slice - squeezed out of water
3 tbsp maida (plain flour)
½ tsp salt
¼ tsp garam masala (mixed spices)
¼ tsp red chilli powder

Vegetable Paneer Kofta ➤

GRAVY

4 tbsp oil
3 onions
2 moti illaichi
½" piece ginger
3 tomatoes - pureed in a mixer
½ cup beaten curd
1 tbsp tomato ketchup
1½ tsp dhania (coriander) powder
½ tsp red chilli powder
½ tsp garam masala
salt to taste

1. Shred all vegetables into thin long strips.
2. Heat 1½ tbsp oil in a karahi. Add capsicum. Fry for a few seconds. Add cabbage & carrot. Stir fry for ½ minute. Add salt and pepper to taste. Remove from fire, cool the filling.

3. Sift maida. Grate paneer. Mix grated paneer, maida and other ingredients of the covering, with the palm of the hand till the grains of the paneer disappear.
4. Divide into 4 big balls. Flatten each ball to a size of about 2½" diameter. Place 1 tbsp of filling in the centre.
5. Lift the sides to cover the filling. Give the kofta an oval shape like an egg.
6. Roll in maida. Deep fry koftas carefully till golden brown.
7. Grind onions, ginger and seeds of moti illaichi together.
8. Grind tomatoes to a puree. Keep aside.
9. Heat 4 tbsp oil in a karahi. Add onion paste and cook on slow fire till golden brown in colour. Add dhania powder. Mix.
10. Add curd gradually, 2-3 tbsp at a time, stirring continuously till all the curd is used.
11. Cook on slow fire till the mixture turns brown again and the oil separates. Add red chilli powder.

12. Add the tomato puree, cook till oil separates.
13. Add enough water to get a thick gravy. Add salt, garam masala, and tomato ketchup and cook covered on slow fire for 5-7 minutes after the first boil. Keep aside.
14. Cut koftas into two, lengthwise. Heat in a preheated oven for 3-4 minutes. Boil the gravy separately, and pour in a serving dish. Arrange the heated koftas on the gravy.
15. Serve immediately.

■

Navratan Curry

Serves 6

250 gms paneer (cottage cheese) - cut into cubes
2 small potatoes
½ cup shelled peas
2 small carrots
1 cup small cauliflower florets
12 french beans
3 big tomatoes - pureed in a mixer
2 big onions
6 flakes garlic
1" piece ginger
2 green chillies
1 tsp chilli powder
1 tsp garam masala
1 tsp jeera (cumin seeds) powder

3 cups coconut milk or water
1 tsp saunf (fennel seeds)
juice of ½ lemon
salt to taste
6 tbsp oil

1. Peel potatoes. Cut cauliflower and potatoes into small pieces and deep fry them on medium heat.
2. Cut beans and carrots into small pieces. Mix peas.
3. Grind onion, ginger, green chillies and garlic to a paste.
4. Grind or crush saunf. Heat oil, add saunf immediately and then add onion, ginger and garlic paste.
5. When onion paste turns light brown, add chilli powder, garam masala and jeera powder.
6. Add fresh tomato puree. Fry till oil separates.
7. Add chopped carrots, beans and peas. Cook for 2 minutes.
8. Add coconut milk or water and cook till the vegetables are done. Add salt.

9. Add paneer, fried potatoes and cauliflower.
10. When the gravy thickens squeeze in lime juice.
11. Garnish with coriander leaves and serve hot.

■

Mattar Paneer

Serves 4

250 gms paneer - cut into 1" cubes
1 cup shelled peas
2 onions
1" piece ginger
3 tomatoes
seeds of 1 moti illaichi (brown cardamoms)
2 cloves (laung)
¼ cup well beaten curd or malai
1 tsp dhania (coriander) powder
½ tsp red chilli powder
½ tsp garam masala
3 tbsp ghee or 4-5 tbsp oil

1. Deep fry paneer to a golden brown colour.
2. Grind onions, ginger, laung, moti illaichi and tomatoes to a puree in a mixer.
3. Heat ghee. Add the onion - tomato puree. Cook till thick and dry. Reduce heat and cook till ghee separates.
4. Add well beaten malai or curd, cook till ghee separates again.
5. Add red chilli powder and dhania powder.
6. Add peas, cook for 1 minute.
7. Add enough water to get a thick gravy. Add salt to taste.
8. Cook covered till peas are done.
9. Add paneer and garam masala.
10. Cook on low heat for 3-4 minutes till paneer gets soft and ghee separates.
11. Serve sprinkled with 1 tsp of beaten curd, chopped coriander and 1 tsp of melon seeds.

Khoya Paneer

Serves 4
150 gms khoya (dried whole milk)
250 gms paneer - cut into 1" cubes
½" ginger piece
2 green chillies
½ tsp jeera (cumin seeds)
a few cashewnuts
2 onions
2 tomatoes - pureed
1 tsp salt
¼ tsp red chilli powder
¼ tsp garam masala
1 cup water
2 tbsp ghee

1. Fry paneer to a golden brown colour.
2. Grind green chillies, ginger and jeera to a fine paste.
3. Grind onions separately.
4. Heat ghee. Add onions. Cook until onions turn light brown.
5. Add mashed khoya. Cook on low heat until khoya turns light brown.
6. Add ginger paste. Cook for 1 minute.
7. Add cashewnuts. Cook for ½ minute.
8. Add tomato puree. Cook until ghee separates.
9. Add water, salt, chillies and garam masala.
10. Boil. Cook on low heat till the gravy is thick and ghee separates.
11. Add paneer, cook for a few minutes more.
12. Serve hot, garnished with grated khoya and cashewnuts.

■

Methi Malai Paneer

Serves 4

200 gms paneer (cottage cheese) - cut into small cubes
½ cup shelled, boiled peas
½ stick dalchini (cinnamon)
2 moti illaichi (cardamoms)
3-4 laung (cloves)
1 tbsp cashewnuts
2 tbsp oil
1 onion - grated
¼ tsp white pepper powder
½ cup (75 gms) malai (cream)
4 tbsp kasoori methi (dry fenugreek leaves)
salt to taste
a pinch of sugar
½ cup milk (approx)

1. Crush together dalchini, laung and seeds of moti illaichi on a chakla-belan. Keep the masala aside.
2. Grind cashewnuts separately on the chakla-belan or in a small spice grinder.
3. Heat oil. Add grated onion and cook on low heat till oil separates. Do not let the onions turn brown.
4. Add the crushed masala and pepper powder. Cook for a few seconds.
5. Add kasoori methi and malai, cook on low heat for 2-3 minutes till malai dries up.
6. Add boiled peas and paneer.
7. Add powdered cashewnuts and cook for a few seconds.
8. Add enough milk to get a thick gravy.
9. Add salt and sugar to taste.
10. Serve with a few peas in the centre, surrounded by a ring of cashewnut bits.

Stuffed Tomatoes

Serves 6

6 firm big tomatoes
2 tbsp bread crumbs
2 onions - finely chopped
2 green chillies - finely chopped
250 gms paneer (cottage cheese) - mashed
salt to taste
3 tbsp oil
½ tsp tandoori masala
few boiled peas

1. Cut tomatoes into two pieces and scoop out each piece. Keep pulp aside.
2. Apply little salt on the inner side of all the pieces of tomatoes.
3. Keep them upside down for a few minutes.
4. Heat oil. Add onions. Cook till transparent.
5. Add tomato pulp and green chillies. Cook till dry.
6. Add mashed paneer, salt and tandoori masala. Cool the filling.
7. Put the filling in the scooped halves. Press.
8. Sprinkle bread crumbs.
9. Put in a greased tray and bake for 8-10 minutes. Alternately, put 2 tbsp oil in a flat bottomed karahi and place the stuffed tomatoes. Cover and cook on low heat for a few minutes. Do not let the tomatoes turn limp.
10. Dot with a boiled pea or a coriander leaf and serve hot.

■

Spinach - Paneer Casserole

Serves 8

200 gms paneer - cut into 1" thin squares
1 kg paalak (spinach)
¼ tsp mitha soda (soda-bicarb)
1 tomato
3/4 tsp salt
½ tsp pepper
1 tsp sugar
2 tbsp butter
½ cup milk
2 laung (cloves) - crushed
1 moti illaichi (brown cardamom) - crushed

TOMATO LAYER
1 onion - finely chopped

1 green chilli - finely chopped
2 flakes garlic - chopped
2 tomatoes - finely chopped
1 tbsp maida (plain flour)
1 tbsp tomato ketchup
1 tbsp oil
½ cup water
salt, pepper to taste

1. Boil paalak with soda-bicarb. Blend paalak and a tomato to a puree in a mixer.
2. Add salt, pepper, sugar, butter, milk, laung and illaichi to paalak & cook till thick and dry. Keep aside.
3. Heat 1 tbsp oil a karahi. Add onion, chilli, garlic and ginger. Cook till onions turn light brown.
4. Add maida. Cook for ½ minute. Add water, stirring continuously.
5. Add tomatoes, salt, pepper and tomato ketchup. Cook for 4-5 minutes till thick.

6. Grease an oven proof dish. Spread half of the paalak. (½" thick layer).
7. Spread half of the tomato mixture on it.
8. Spread half of the paneer on the tomato layer.
9. Put a layer of paalak again, then paneer and lastly tomatoes.
10. Sprinkle some bread crumbs.
11. Bake till golden brown. Grate some paneer on top. Serve hot.

■

Paneer Tawa Masala

Serves 4

**300 gms paneer (cottage cheese) slab - cut into ½" thick rectangle
of size - 8" x 3" approx. (get the paneer block cut horizontally
when purchasing paneer)
2 capsicums
2 onions
1 firm tomato
1 cup (200 gms) curd of full cream milk
3/4 tsp salt
½ tsp red chilli powder
¼ tsp orange red colour**

**DRY MASALA
5-6 chhoti illaichi (green cardamoms)
3-4 sticks dalchini (cinnamon)
8-10 laung (cloves), 1 tsp ajwain (carom seeds)**

1. Grind chhoti illaichi, laung, dalchini and ajwain together. Keep this dry masala aside.
2. Hang the curd in a fine muslin cloth for 15 minutes.
3. Add salt, chilli powder and enough colour to give the curd a bright orange colour.
4. Cover the paneer slab with this curd and keep in a greased tray for atleast 15-20 minutes.
5. Heat the oven to 200°C. Keep the paneer which is marinated in curd in a preheated oven for 10-15 minutes or till the curd dries up and forms a coating.
6. Turn the paneer carefully with a sharp spatula.
7. Keep it in the oven for 5-7 minutes if it is wet on this side.
8. Remove from the oven and keep aside.
9. Cut each capsicum into 8 pieces to get 1" pieces of capsicum. Cut each onion into four pieces and separate the onion leaves. Cut tomatoes into 8 pieces. Remove pulp.

10. Heat 1½ tbsp oil in a non-stick pan. Add 1 tsp of the prepared dry masala powder.
11. Immediately put the slab of paneer. Cook on low heat for 1 minute. Do not let it turn black.
12. Turn the slab again. Remove from pan. Keep aside.
13. At the time of serving, keep the paneer in a hot oven for 5-7 minutes till it gets soft and heated properly or microwave for 2 minutes.
14. In the meantime, heat 2 tbsp oil in the pan, add 1 tsp dry masala powder, add the capsicum & onions immediately. Cook for 2-3 minutes. Add tomatoes, sprinkle ½ tsp salt on the vegetables. Mix well.
15. Serve these vegetables around the heated paneer kept in a flat serving dish.
16. Give cuts to the paneer slab diagonally, 1" apart, and then a cross cut, keeping the slab together.

Paalak-Paneer

Serves 4

150 gms paneer - cut into 1" cubes and deep fried
½ kg paalak (spinach) with small leaves
2 onions
1" piece ginger
5-6 flakes garlic - optional
2 tomatoes - chopped
2 green chillies - chopped
2-3 tbsp ghee
salt to taste
seeds of 2 moti illaichi (brown cardamom) - crushed

1. Wash, chop, paalak. Pressure cook with ½ cup water for 10 minutes on low heat after the first whistle.
2. Cool. Grind to a smooth paste.
3. Grind onions, garlic & ginger together.
4. Heat ghee. Add onions paste. Cook till onions turn golden brown and ghee separates.
5. Add chopped tomatoes and green chillies. Cook for 5-6 minutes on slow fire, till ghee separates.
6. Add the ground paalak, add a little water if too thick.
7. Cook for 5-7 minutes on slow fire. Add salt.
8. Add illaichi and paneer. Mix well. Remove from fire.
9. At the time of serving, heat 1 tbsp ghee, add 1 tsp red chilli powder. Remove from fire and pour this baghar over the heated paalak. Mix well. Serve at once.

■

Methi Chaman

Serves 2

100 gms paalak (spinach)
50 gms methi (fenugreek leaves)
½ potato - cut into long fingers
75 gms paneer (cottage cheese)
3 tbsp ghee
¼" piece ginger
oil for frying
½ tsp haldi (turmeric)
1 tsp salt
1 tsp dhania (coriander) powder
3/4 tsp red chilli powder
½ tsp kashmiri garam masala
1 cup water
seeds of 2 moti illaichi - crushed

1. Cut paneer into 1½" cubes. Deep fry and keep aside.
2. Cut the potato into long fingers and deep fry.
3. Wash and grind methi leaves, paalak and ginger together with a little water. Heat the ghee, add the ground mixture and fry for about 15 minutes, till it is dry and separates from ghee.
4. Add salt, haldi, dhania powder and red chilli powder. Cook for 2-3 minutes.
5. Add the fried potato fingers. Cook for 1 minute. Add water.
6. Simmer on slow fire till the potato fingers are cooked and the ghee separates.
7. Add fried paneer and moti illaichi. Sprinkle kashmiri garam masala. Serve hot.

■

Tandoori Paneer

Serves 4

250 gms paneer - cut into cubes
3-4 flakes garlic - optional
1" piece ginger
2-3 green chillies
1 tsp jeera (cumin seeds)
3/4 tsp salt
¼ tsp red chilli powder
orange red colour
1 tomato - pureed or blanched
2 capsicums - cut into rings
2 onions - cut into rings
1 heaped tbsp ghee

1. Grind garlic, ginger, jeera & green chillies to a fine paste.
2. Add salt & chilli powder to the paste. Add enough orange colour to give a bright colour to the paste.
3. Cut paneer into 1" squares. Apply this paste nicely on all the pieces.
4. Put this paneer in a greased dish and grill for 10 minutes till it is dry and slightly crisp.
   Alternately, paneer can be left like this (marinated) for 1 hour till dry.
5. Heat 1 heaped tbsp ghee in a karahi. Fry onion & capsicum rings for a few minutes till onions get transparent. Keep aside a few capsicum rings.
6. Add tomato puree & cook till dry.
7. Add ½ tsp salt and paneer pieces. Toss for a minute. Serve immediately, garnished with capsicum rings.

■

Badam Paneer Curry

Serves 4

200 gms paneer - cut into small cubes
2 onions
½" ginger piece
1 tsp bhuna jeera (roasted cumin seeds) powder
1 tbsp khus-khus (poppy seeds)
1 tbsp broken cashewnuts
½ tsp chilli powder
salt to taste
1 tsp garam masala
1 cup coconut milk
2 tbsp curd
3 tbsp cream or well beaten malai
4 tbsp ghee
10 badam (almonds)

1. Cut paneer into ¼" (tiny) square pieces.
2. Grind onion and ginger to a paste.
3. Grind cashewnuts and khus-khus together.
4. Blanch and split almonds.
5. Heat ghee. Fry almonds to a golden brown colour. Remove from ghee. Keep aside.
6. Add onions paste to ghee. Cook till golden brown in colour.
7. Add cashewnut paste. Cook for 1-2 minutes.
8. Add chilli powder and jeera.
9. Add curd and cook till ghee separates.
10. Add coconut milk and salt. Cook for 5-7 minutes.
11. Add garam masala and cream.
12. Remove from fire.
13. Add paneer at the time of serving.

■

Keema Paneer

Serves 4

250 gms paneer - mashed
1 cup shelled, boiled peas
1 tsp jeera (cumin seeds)
1 tsp red chilli powder, ½ tsp garam masala, salt to taste
3 tbsp oil
1 green chilli - chopped finely

1. Mash paneer roughly. Dry the mashed paneer in a clean karahi on low heat for 2-3 minutes. Do not keep it for too long on the fire.
2. Heat oil in a clean karahi. Add jeera. When it splutters, add red chilli powder. Add the peas. Cook for 1 minute.
3. Add the dried paneer, green chillies and garam masala.
4. Cook for a few seconds. Serve hot.

Snacks

Paneer Canapes

Serves 4

2 slices of bread
100 gms paneer - mashed roughly
1 small onion - finely chopped
½ small tomato - pulp removed and finely chopped
1 green chilli - finely chopped
½ tsp roasted jeera powder
½ tsp salt
salted butter
2 tbsp tomato sauce (chilli garlic)
few boiled peas
fresh coriander leaves

1. In a clean karahi, add the mashed paneer and cook on low heat for 1 minute. Remove from fire.
2. Chop onion, tomato and green chilli as finely as possible.
3. Mix onion, tomato, green chilli, salt and jeera powder with the paneer. Keep aside.
4. Toast the slices. Butter them.
5. Cut into four square pieces.
6. Heap a tablespoon full of paneer (prepared as above) on each piece.
7. Dot with chilli garlic sauce and a boiled pea.
8. Serve hot, garnished with a small coriander leaf.

■

Multi Storeyed Pancakes

Serves 4-5   Picture on facing page

1½ cups maida (plain flour)
2¼ - 2½ cups milk
1 tsp salt, ½ tsp pepper, ¼ tsp mitha soda (soda-bicarb)

FILLING
200 gms paneer (cottage cheese) - mashed roughly
1 big boiled potato - mashed coarsely
3 onions - chopped finely, 2 green chillies - chopped finely
¼ tsp haldi (turmeric powder), ½ tsp red chilli powder
salt, pepper to taste
3 tbsp oil

Cheesy Green Toasts : Recipe on page 90 ➤
Multi Storeyed Pancakes ➤

1. Sift maida, salt, soda and pepper.
2. Add milk. Beat well with an egg-beater. Add enough milk to get a pouring consistency.
3. Heat a non-stick pan (not too hot). Smear 1 tsp oil on it in the centre.
4. Remove from fire and pour 1/3 cup (1 big karchi) batter. Tilt the pan to spread the batter. Return to fire.
5. Turn the pancake when the under side is cooked. When the other side is cooked, remove from pan and keep aside.
6. Make 6-7 such pancakes.
7. Cook onions in oil till transparent.
8. Add haldi and red chillies.
9. Add the potatoes. Cook on slow fire for ½ minute.
10. Add paneer and green chillies.
11. Add salt, pepper to taste.
12. Remove from fire. Keep this filling aside.

13. Place a pancake on a greased stainless steel plate.
14. Spread some filling over it.
15. Cover with another pancake. Press well.
16. Repeat in the same way, ending with a pancake. Press well.
17. Cut the stacked pancakes with any round stainless steel box with a sharp edge of about 7-8" diameter, to give the pancakes a neat look.
18. Heat in a preheated oven for only 5-10 minutes before serving. If it is in the oven for a longer period, it tends to get dry. During the waiting period, it should be covered with the steel box to prevent it from becoming extra crisp in the oven.
19. Some processed cheese may be grated on the pancakes before heating them in the oven.

■

Paneer Cutlets

Serves 8-10   *Picture on page 93*

4 tbsp maida (plain flour)
4 tbsp oil
1 cup milk
2 tsp salt
½ tsp pepper
½ tsp red chilli powder
200 gms paneer - grated
5 big boiled potatoes - grated
bread crumbs

1. Heat oil. Cook maida for 1-2 minutes on low heat.
2. Add milk, stirring continuously.
3. Cook till a thick lump is formed. Remove from fire. Add grated paneer.
4. Add mashed or grated boiled potatoes.
5. Mix well. Add salt, pepper and chilli powder.
6. Make balls. Flatten each ball and give it a heart shape.
7. Roll in bread crumbs. Chill the prepared cutlets for some time. Shallow fry in a small quantity of oil in a pan.
8. Serve with boiled vegetables sauted in a little butter.

∎

Note: Dip the cutlet in one egg white mixed with 1 tbsp water, then roll in bread crumbs and shallow fry. This gives a thicker outer covering to the cutlet.

Paneer Sticks

Serves 8

100 gms paneer (cottage cheese)
2 capsicum or ¼ of a small cabbage
2 small onions, 2 small tomatoes (firm)
a few toothpicks
½ tsp salt, ½ tsp red chilli powder
2-3 sticks dalchini (cinnamon)
4-5 laung (cloves), ½ tsp ajwain (omum)
4-5 chhoti illaichi (green cardamoms)

1. Cut capsicum into 3/4" square pieces, removing the seeds.
2. Cut onions into four pieces & separate them. Cut tomatoes into four pieces. If they are large, cut into eight pieces.
3. Cut paneer into 3/4" thick cubes.
4. Prepare dry masala powder by grinding together dalchini, laung,

ajwain and chhoti illaichi to a coarse powder.
(Larger quantity of the masalas can be ground together & stored in an air tight container for future use).

5. Heat 1 tbsp oil in a non-stick pan. Remove from fire.
6. Add 3/4 tsp of the prepared masala powder.
7. Add the paneer cubes. Add red chilli powder and salt to taste. Cook on fire for 2 minutes. Remove from pan and keep aside.
8. Heat 1 tbsp oil again. Add 1 tsp of masala. Add capsicum & onions. Toss for a few seconds. Add salt to taste.
9. Add the tomatoes. Sprinkle ½ tsp more masala. Mix.
10. Remove vegetables from the pan.
11. Take a toothpick. Insert a capsicum piece, then a paneer cube, next onion and lastly a tomato piece.
12. Anything may be repeated if desired.
13. Arrange such toothpicks and serve hot.
14. The sticks may be made an hour in advance and heated in a hot oven for 3-4 minutes, before serving.

Cheesy Green Toasts

Serves 8   *Picture on page 83*

4 bread slices - toasted
¼ of a small cabbage - chopped finely
2 tbsp tomato ketchup
150 gms paneer (cottage cheese) - cut into thin slices
2 firm small tomatoes - cut into slices
butter enough to spread on 4 slices
salt, pepper to taste

1. Toast slices lightly.
2. Butter a toast.
3. Cover it with slices of paneer.
4. Sprinkle salt, pepper on it.
5. Mix tomato ketchup to chopped cabbage.
6. Sprinkle some cabbage on the paneer slice.
7. Cut the toast into two rectangular halves. Top each half with a tomato slice.
8. Sprinkle salt, pepper.
9. Place in a heated oven for 3-4 minutes for just enough time to heat the toast.
10. Serve hot.

■

Toasted Paneer Sandwiches

Serves 4   *Picture on facing page*

4 bread slices
75-100 gms of paneer (cottage cheese) - cut into thin slices
1 boiled potato - cut into thin slices
2 leaves of cabbage
1 firm tomato - cut into slices
½ cucumber - cut into slices
1 tbsp vinegar
½ tsp sugar
½ tsp salt
salted butter - enough for 4 slices

Paneer Cutlet : Recipe on page 86 ➢
Toasted Paneer Sandwiches ➢

1. Pickle cucumber by dipping in vinegar to which 1 tbsp water, salt and sugar has been added. Keep on fire for ½ minute.
2. Dip cabbage leaves in salted boiling water. Remove immediately, wipe dry.
3. Heat butter in a non-stick pan. Toss potatoes and paneer slices in it. Toast slices.
4. Butter one toast. Keep a cabbage leaf to cover the toast.
5. Cover with paneer slices. Sprinkle salt and pepper.
6. Top the paneer with potato slices and then tomato slices.
7. Top it with pickled cucumber. Sprinkle salt and pepper.
8. Place a buttered toast and press gently.
9. Pass a very tiny piece of tomato and capsicum through two tooth picks to make them look pretty.
10. Cut the sandwich into two, pass the tooth picks to hold the sandwiches together. Serve with potato wafers.

■

Paneer Dosa with Cream

Serves 8

1½ cups uncooked rice (ordinary quality)
½ cup dhuli urad dal (split black beans)
1 tsp salt
1 tsp methi dana (fenugreek seeds)
1 tsp sugar

FILLING
250 gms paneer
2 onions - chopped fine
1 tsp rai (mustard seeds)
2-3 green chillies - chopped
salt to taste
½ tsp haldi (turmeric powder)
¼ tsp red chilli powder

3-4 tbsp oil
2-3 whole dried red chillies broken into bits
50 gms thick cream

1. Soak dal with methi dana, and rice separately for 10-12 hours.
2. Grind both separately.
3. Mix the two together. Add salt.
4. The batter should be of pouring consistency, but not very thin, so add water accordingly.
5. Keep the batter in a warm place for 8-10 hours to ferment. If the batter does not rise, add ½ tsp soda-bicarb at the time of making dosa and mix well.
6. Add sugar to the batter at the time of making the dosas.
7. Heat oil in a karahi.
8. Add mustard seeds & red chillies.
9. When they splutter, add onions. Cook till transparent.
10. Add haldi, chilli powder & salt.

11. Add mashed paneer and green chillies. Cook for 3-4 minutes. Keep the filling aside.
12. Heat a nonstick pan. Smear 1 tsp oil in the centre. Remove from fire. Put ½ katori (½ cup) batter and spread immediately with bottom part of the katori.
13. Now put 1-2 tbsp of oil on the dosa & the sides.
14. When the under side gets cooked, place the filling, spread 1 tbsp of thick cream on the filling. Fold to overlap the sides.
15. Serve hot with coconut chutney and sambhar.

■

Paneer Mushroom Turnovers

Serves 15

200 gms maida (plain flour)
100 gms salted butter
pinch of salt
pinch of baking powder
7 tsp cold water
½ tsp ajwain (carom seeds)

FILLING
1 onion
150 gms paneer - mashed
75 gms mushrooms
¼" piece ginger - finely chopped
1 green chilli - finely chopped
salt & masalas to taste
2 tbsp oil

1. Sift maida, salt and baking powder. Add ajwain.
2. Cut butter into small pieces and rub it gently with your finger tips into the maida till it starts resembling fine bread crumbs.
3. Make a dough with ice cold water with minimum handling. Knead lightly. Wrap in a damp cloth. Chill the dough for at least 15-20 minutes.
4. Fry ginger, mushrooms and onion in oil till onions turn transparent. Add green chillies & paneer.
5. Add salt & masalas to taste.
6. Cook for 1 minute. Keep the filling aside.
7. Make marble sized balls of the dough.
8. Roll each into 2½ inches diameter.
9. Place the prepared filling on one side & fold the other side over it. Seal using a fork. Brush with milk.
10. Bake for 15-20 minutes at 200°C in a preheated oven.

■

Potato Loaf

Serves 4

4-5 boiled potatoes - mashed
3 slices of bread - squeezed out of water
1 bunch coriander - chopped
salt, pepper to taste
spices - red chilli powder, amchoor and garam masala to taste
bread crumbs or thin seviyan to coat

FILLING
150 gms paneer - mashed
1 green chilli - chopped finely, 1 onion - chopped finely
1 tbsp chopped coriander
½ tsp each of garam masala, haldi and red chilli powder
½ cup boiled peas
2 tbsp oil

1. Heat oil. Cook onions till transparent.
2. Add haldi, red chilli powder and peas.
3. Add paneer, green chillies and coriander. Add salt to taste.
4. Remove from fire after stirring for 1 minute. Keep filling aside.
5. Mix potatoes, bread, coriander and all the spices.
6. Make a ball of the potato mixture. Place on a greased rectangular tray and flatten it to a rectangular shape, about ½" thick.
7. Place a row of filling in the centre.
8. Pick up the sides of the potato mixture to cover the filling and make a rectangular loaf of about 2" height.
9. Coat with bread crumbs or thin seviyan.
10. Shallow fry the loaf very carefully in a frying pan, using two flat spoons for turning the loaf. Drain on absorbent paper.

■

Moong Dal Chillahs with Paneer

Serves 4   Picture on facing page

1 cup moong dal (split green gram)
½ tsp salt, ½ tsp red chilli powder
150-200 gms paneer (cottage cheese) - cut into 3" long fingers
2 tbsp oil, ½ tsp salt
½ tsp garam masala, ½ tsp red chilli powder

1. Soak dal for 3-4 hours only. Do not soak for a longer period.
2. Strain. Grind with 1 cup water to a smooth batter. Add about ½ cup water to get a pouring consistency.
3. Add ½ tsp salt and ½ tsp chilli powder. Keep aside.
4. Prepare the paneer by heating 2 tbsp oil in a non-stick pan. Add ½ tsp salt, ½ tsp garam masala and ½ tsp red chilli powder. Shut off the gas.

Moong Dal Chillahs with Paneer ➤

5. Add paneer pieces and mix gently with the oil.
6. Return to fire, fry for a few seconds. Remove from pan. Keep aside.
7. Heat a non-stick pan (not too hot), smear 1 tsp oil in the centre.
8. Spread one karchi (¼ cup) of batter to make a chillah of about 4" diameter.
9. Pour some oil on the sides.
10. Turn over.
11. Heat one prepared paneer piece on the side of the pan.
12. Remove chillah and paneer from the pan.
13. Place the paneer piece at one end of the chillah. Roll it up.
14. Serve hot with poodina chutney or any other sauce.
15. To make the next chillah, put off the gas. Cool the pan by sprinkling some water. Wipe clean.
16. Smear 1 tsp oil in the centre. Spread a karchi of batter.
17. Return to fire and proceed as before.

Cocktail Paneer Samosa

Serves 10

3/4 cup maida (plain flour)
¼ cup suji (semolina)
a pinch of baking powder
¼ tsp salt
2 semi heaped tbsp of ghee (vansapati) or margarine

FILLING
200 gms paneer - grated
2 small boiled potatoes - mashed coarsely
3 tbsp oil
¼" piece ginger - finely chopped
½ tsp red chilli powder
salt to taste
3/4 tsp roasted jeera (cumin seeds) powder

3/4 tsp garam masala
¼ tsp amchoor (dried mango powder)
1 tbsp kaju (cashewnuts) bits
1 tbsp kishmish (raisins)
2 green chillies - finely chopped
¼ tsp sugar

1. Mix maida, suji, salt, baking powder and ghee.
2. Add a few tbsp of water and knead to form a stiff dough.
3. Keep covered for ½ hour.
4. Heat oil. Put off the fire. Add ginger. Add salt, red chilli powder, garam masala, jeera, and amchoor. Return to fire.
5. Add nuts. Cook for a few seconds.
6. Add potatoes. Cook for ½ minute.
7. Add paneer. Mix well. Add sugar and green chillies.
8. Cover and cook on slow fire for 3-4 minutes. Make the filling spicy. Keep aside.

9. Make marble sized balls of the dough.
10. Roll out thinly. Cut into two.
11. Fold each half into a triangle to form a cone.
12. Seal the cone by applying water. Fill 1 tbsp of the filling inside the cone.
13. Make a small fold or plate on the joint of the cone.
14. Now close the cone with water. Press the side opposite to the pointed side against a plate, giving it a samosa look.
15. Heat oil. Deep fry 8-10 pieces at a time on slow fire.

■

Paneer Pakora

Serves 10

400 gms paneer (cottage cheese)
1½ cups besan (gram flour)
2 pinches of mitha soda or baking powder
1 tsp salt
1 tsp red chilli powder
¼ tsp ajwain (carom seeds)
1 cup milk (approx)

FILLING
1¼ tsp salt
1½ tsp red chilli powder
1½ tsp garam masala
1½ tsp dhania (coriander) powder
4-5 tsp lemon juice

1. Mix besan, salt, red chilli, ajwain and soda or baking powder.
2. Add enough milk gradually, to get a thick batter.
3. Beat the batter well till light.
4. Mix all ingredients of the filling, adding enough lemon juice to make a thick paste.
5. Cut paneer into slices which are slightly thicker than ¼".
6. Cut these slices into 1½" square pieces.
7. Slit the paneer piece half way, not till the end.
8. Insert a little filling in the slit with the help of a knife. Repeat with other paneer pieces.
9. If any filling is left over, apply it on the surface of the paneer pieces.
10. Heat oil. Dip paneer pieces in batter and deep fry on medium fire to a golden brown colour.
11. Serve hot with poodina chutney to which a little imli ki chutney is also mixed.

■

Paneer Roll Ups

Serves 12
5 tbsp maida (plain flour)
2 small eggs
¼ tsp salt
¼ tsp pepper
½ cup milk - approx.

FILLING
200 gms paneer (cottage cheese) - mashed
2 small capsicums - chopped finely
1 big onion - chopped finely
2 green chillies - chopped finely
1 tsp red chilli powder
½ tsp garam masala
salt to taste
1 tbsp oil

1. Beat maida, eggs, salt, pepper and milk together to get a smooth batter of a very thin pouring consistency.
2. Heat a non-stick pan. Smear 1 tsp oil in the centre.
3. Remove from fire and pour one karchi (1/3 cup) of batter. Spread by tilting the pan. Cook on slow fire.
5. When the underside is cooked, remove from the pan on to a plate. Keep aside.
6. Cook onions and capsicum in oil till onions turn pink.
7. Add paneer and green chillies.
8. Add salt, red chilli powder & garam masala. Cook for 1 minute.
9. Remove from fire & cool.
10. Cut 1½" strip from two sides of the pancake. Keep the strips aside.
11. Cut the left over pancake into two equal pieces length wise.
12. Place the 1½" strip on the edge of one piece.
13. Put 1 tbsp full of the filling in the centre of the strip.

14. Fold the sides of the strip to cover the filling.
15. Roll the pancake tightly. Keep aside.
16. Similarly prepare the second roll with the second piece of pancake.
17. Fry in very little oil in a pan on slow fire. Serve hot on a bed of open cabbage leaves and thickly sliced capsicums.

■

Note: Do not let the roll-ups turn brown on frying, so do not heat the oil too much at the time of frying.

Chaawal - Roti

Tandoori Paneer Parantha

Serves 4
2 cups (250 gms) atta (whole wheat flour)
1 cup (200 ml) water - approx.
½ tsp salt, 2-3 tbsp solid ghee
kasoori methi (dry fenugreek leaves)

FILLING
100 gms paneer - mashed
1 onion - chopped finely
1 green chilli - chopped finely
3/4 tsp salt, 3/4 tsp red chilli powder
3/4 tsp garam masala

1. Keep ghee in the fridge for some time, so that it solidifies.
2. Make a soft dough with atta, salt and water. Keep aside for ½ hour.

3. Mix all ingredients of the filling. Keep aside.
4. Divide the dough into 6 equal parts. Shape into round balls.
5. Flatten each ball, roll out each into a round of 5" diameter.
6. Spread 1 tsp full of solidifide ghee. Then spread 1 tbsp of filling all over.
7. Make a slit, starting from the centre till any one end.
8. Start rolling from the slit, to form an even cone.
9. Keeping the cone upright, press slightly.
10. Roll out, applying pressure only at the centre. Do not roll or press two much on the sides, otherwise the layers of parantha do not separate after cooking.
11. Sprinkle some kasoori methi and press with a rolling pin (belan).
12. Apply water on the back side of the paratha and stick carefully in a heated tandoor or place in a preheated oven in a greased tray.
13. Remove after a few minutes.
14. Spread some ghee, serve hot.

Paneer Biryani

Serves 5-6

2 cups Basmati rice
200 gms paneer - cut into 1" cubes
2 onions - sliced finely
½ cup oil, 3 tsp salt
1 tsp lemon juice, 1 tej patta (bay leaf)

PASTE
6-7 flakes garlic, 1" piece ginger
1 tbsp saunf (aniseeds), 1 tsp jeera (cumin seeds)
3 dried whole red chillies
1 tsp saboot dhania (coriander seeds)
1 stick of dalchini (cinnamon), 3-4 laung (cloves)
3-4 saboot kali mirch (peppercorns)
1-2 moti illaichi (brown cardamoms)

1. Soak rice for 1 hour.
2. Grind the ingredients of the paste together with a little water.
3. Fry paneer to a golden brown colour.
4. Heat oil in a heavy bottomed pan. Add onions, cook till golden brown.
5. Add the paste and tej patta and stir fry for 1-2 minutes.
6. Add the fried paneer. Add 4 cups of water.
7. Add salt & lemon juice.
8. When water boils, strain the rice and add to the water.
9. Put a tawa under the pan of rice.
10. Cover the pan of rice with a small towel napkin and then with a well fitting lid. Keep some heavy weight on the lid.
11. Slow down the fire and cook till the rice is done (10-15 minutes).

■

Paneer Bhature

Serves 4

2 cups (250 gms) maida (plain flour)
1 cup (100 gms) suji (semolina)
½ tsp soda-bicarb
½ tsp salt
1 tsp sugar
½ cup sour curd (approx)
oil for deep frying

FILLING
75 gms paneer - mashed
½ tsp salt
3/4 tsp red chilli powder
½ tsp garam masala

1. Soak suji in water, which is just enough to cover it.
2. Sift salt, soda and maida. Add sugar, curd and the soaked suji. Knead with enough warm water to make a dough of rolling consistency.
3. Knead again with greased hands till the dough is smooth.
4. Brush the dough with oil.
5. Keep the dough in a greased polythene and keep it in a warm place for 3-4 hours.
6. Make 8-10 balls. Roll out, put 1 tbsp of filling. Cover the filling with the dough to form a ball again.
7. Roll each ball to an oblong shape, and deep fry in hot oil.

■

Paneer Nan

Serves 6-8

3 cups (300 gms) maida (plain flour)
½ cup curd
½ cup warm water - approx.
1 tsp salt
4 tsp sugar
4 tsp oil
1 tsp kalaunji (onion seeds)
1 tsp khus-khus (poppy seeds)
1 tsp mitha soda (soda-bicarb)

FILLING
100 gms paneer - mashed
1 onion - finely chopped, 1 green chilli - chopped
salt, red chilli powder, garam masala to taste

1. Sift maida and salt. Add sugar.
2. Mix curd and oil. Knead with enough water to a dough.
3. Mix 1 tsp of soda bicarb in ½ tbsp hot water and sprinkle on the kneaded dough. Knead again with a little oil to a make a soft dough. Brush with oil.
4. Keep in a warm place for 3-4 hours.
5. Mix all ingredients of the filling.
6. Make 6-8 balls.
7. Roll out each ball. Place 1 tbsp of filling.
8. Lift the sides to cover the filling.
9. Roll out again. Sprinkle some kalaunji and khus-khus. Roll in an oblong shape.
10. Apply some water on the back side of the nan. Stick in a hot tandoor.
11. Cook till nan is ready.

■

Mushroom & Paneer Pullao

Serves 4

1 cup Basmati rice
100 gms mushrooms (½ packet)
150 gms paneer (cottage cheese)
1 onion
1 carrot - optional
1 capsicum - optional
2-3 laung (cloves)
1 stick dalchini (cinnamon)
1½ tsp salt
2 tbsp desi ghee or 3 tbsp oil

1. Clean, wash rice. Soak for 1 hour.
2. Wash mushrooms thoroughly and cut each into thick slices lengthwise, into 'T' shaped pieces.
3. Cut paneer into ½" square pieces and deep fry to a golden colour.
4. Shred the carrot and capsicum into thin strips.
5. Heat ghee. Add dalchini, laung and onions. Cook till onions turn light brown in colour.
6. Add mushrooms. Cook for 3-4 minutes on slow fire.
7. Add 2 cups of water. Add the rice, capsicum and carrot. Add paneer.
8. Add salt. Boil.
9. Cook covered on slow fire till the rice is done.

■

Paneer Shashlik

2 cups rice (soaked for 1 hour)
1 onion - sliced finely
3-4 laung (cloves)
½ tsp red chilli powder
1½ tsp salt
3 tbsp oil

DIP
1 cup curd
2 tbsp tandoori masala
½" piece ginger & 2 green chillies - ground to a paste together

SAUCE
3 big onions
5-6 flakes garlic
½" piece ginger